I0428470

Texas

Bigfoot

In My Backyard

Short Stories Volume Two

DAWN

Goes Missing

Susan Sullivan

Texas Bigfoot In My Backyard

Short Stories Series Volume Two
DAWN Goes Missing

Published by Purple Sage Publishing

Copyright 2014 by Susan Sullivan

All rights reserved. No part of this book may be reproduced or transmitted in any form or by any means, electronic or mechanical, including photocopying and recording, or by any information storage and retrieval system, without permission in writing from the author and the publisher.

ISBN-13:978-1503220379
ISBN-10:1503220370

DEDICATION

This book is dedicated to all the readers and reviewers and now e-mailers who read the first books. Especially to those who have emailed me and shared their own personal experiences, opinions and beliefs. They have become my lifelong friends and confidants. I received so much positive feedback from them that I decided to continue to share more short stories of my personal experiences of my life here on The Bigfoot Ranch In Texas.

I would also like to dedicate this book to my good friend, Pat, who was the first person to read my books. She was also the librarian at the junior high where I worked in the afterschool program. She allowed me the opportunity to donate five books to the library. She cataloged and coded the books and placed them on the shelf so the students could check out my books. She and I also created

AR tests so the students could also earn reading points. Remember, the only reason I wrote the book in the first place was to share my story with my students. Pat gave me the opportunity to accomplish my goal, I could not have done it without her.

This book is dedicated to my husband and children who still continue to live these experiences with me till this very day. I also dedicate this book to our visitors who still live somewhere out there and still come to visit our house on a weekly basis. I also dedicate this book to the hundreds of individuals who now feel it is okay to share their own experiences with me, without judgment, without persecution and without ridicule. This is for you.

Table of Contents

PROLOGUE

Thank you once again for continuing on this journey with me. I must admit our experiences have become stranger and unexpectedly paranormal. I will get to those experiences in later volumes. This book however continues where we ended in the last Short Stories Book, Volume One Memories.

Remember we left off with the dogs, Wendy and Pickles being taught to fetch by some unforeseen force or visitor. (Or was it just raining balls?) Well, this is where we left off. If you read the last book, please forgive me, and please allow me to recap what has happened for those who did not read the previous book. I promise to be short and to the point.

We began to notice tennis balls and baseballs appearing in the yard. We assumed they were ours and were shocked when I checked my ball hopper in the garage and it was secure, not a ball missing. This was when we realized that something was coming to the ranch with balls in hand and throwing them at the dogs in an attempt to teach them to fetch. This was all based on our opinion and experiences on the ranch, and having already dealt with the Sasquatches on the ranch for two years.

Before the holidays my husband had discussed his desire to acquire a new puppy, one who could fetch. He had begun his research and had planned to purchase a Golden Retriever for Christmas. We assumed the Sasquatches heard us and were desperately trying to teach the dogs to fetch since they were about to be replaced. (So they thought.) This was when the tennis balls and baseballs started showing up in the yard. We had no plans to get rid of the other two dogs. We had always planned to add to our growing family.

Unfortunately due to the increasingly strange activity on the ranch, we postponed our purchase. Things were beyond our control and we really did not feel right bringing another animal into this situation.

So this is where we are. We have been living on the ranch for two whole years. This book takes us into new experiences that we have had in the beginning of the third year. We are still discovering deeper and more paranormal aspects of this phenomena. This year is different. I have new friends who are going on this journey with me. There is Mark from Ohio, Patty, Molly and Lori, and then there is Mike. I met some through Twitter, some were readers, and then some are actual Habituators. We were brought together by mutual friends. I am so grateful to these new friends of mine who have allowed me to share experiences that I may never speak of in person or in public. They make me feel so sane and so normal. I know I can email, and yes call them on the phone at a moment's notice if I need a friend. Then there is my sweet little new puppy who makes me laugh every day.

Chapter One
The New Puppy

Yes, you read that right. No, we did not buy a new puppy. If you by chance are well read in everything Bigfoot/Sasquatch, and I don't mean mainstream books, then you will understand what I am talking about in a few minutes. If you are well read in the Bigfoot/Sasquatch phenomena and the other mysterious aspects of Bigfoot, then you will definitely understand.

We had an event, an experience that I am still having to come to terms with till this day. I do plan to tell you all about it, but not yet. I will just tell you that I was furious. I was prepared to move away from the ranch and go back to the big city. After all we still have a house in Dallas and a house in New Mexico. We could move again at a moment's notice and still land on our feet.

I was so mad. What we experienced I would not wish upon my worst enemies. Well, maybe one or two. (Just kidding!) I was so upset I had decided to call my next book, The Last Book! I was done with all of this Bigfoot/Sasquatch nonsense and I was not about to add to the already unpredictable situation by bringing another animal to the ranch. I was so upset I could not focus on The Second Year book. (If you are wondering why that book had been delayed, that is why.) Then came Sparky.

If you read Angels and Bigfoot, you will remember I talked about the small puppy my husband had just rescued. He was sitting at my feet, chin on my toes, under my desk as I finished my book. I had run into my husband at the local Walmart the night before. By local I mean we both happened to run into each other at a store that was over twenty five miles away. So I was surprised to see my husband, but I was not surprised to see him with a cart full of dog toys, puppy chow, dog bowls, doggie bed, leashes, shampoo, collars, and carpet powder, carpet shampoo and I think there might have been something in there for me to soften the blow. Yes, we had our new puppy.

That day my husband had taken the boys to Karate class. The Karate Master had rescued a puppy that she had found on the highway near the school. She asked if we could take it and give it a home and my husband could not refuse. He brought the black little puppy home. My youngest son named him Sparky. At the time he looked as though he might have been a six week old half Black Lab and half Pit Bull. We were not happy when he started biting my boys and exhibiting aggressive behavior towards my sons. His jaws were getting bigger and bigger. We were devastated when we thought we had brought home a full blooded Pit Bull puppy. He began to chew and bite the other animals, blankets, toys, and us. He terrorized the cats. So, we began to look for a suitable home for the puppy. I immediately found a student whose parents were familiar with Pit Bulls and had raised them as well, and were looking for a new dog. Then for some reason I changed my mind and made the decision to keep him even if he was a Pit Bull. I figured if anyone could handle living on the ranch, he could. I had also fallen in love with those big black eyes, and he became mine. Besides, I figured it was all a matter of training and teaching him not to bite. (Still working on it!!)

I now call him Spartacus. We once had a gorgeous Great Pyrenees named Samson, yes from the Bible. It is amazing how we honor and remember and even celebrate characters from ancient history, Biblical characters, legends and mythology, yet we totally discount anything from Native American mythology such as Sasquatch and the Tribes of Giants that have been spoken about among many North American tribes. No they didn't have marble columns and Greek and Roman Temples, instead they had the redwoods and the mighty North American Forest. No they didn't have statues, instead they had totem poles and petroglyphs. One day they will have their rightful place in history.

Chapter Two
The Sasquatch's Puppy

There was something definitely different about Spartacus. He was different than the other two dogs. He loved being outside. The other dogs were terrified and hated being outside. The other two have been with us for almost two years. We lost one dog who wondered down the road and was hit by a car. I remember the day. I am so glad I did not see it, because I know I would have fallen apart.

I noticed someone pulled over along the side of the road close to the ranch as I was driving down the highway on my way home from work. They were looking for something in the grass along the roadside. I had no idea it had anything to do with my dog. Then I pulled off onto my road and then down my half mile driveway. About five minutes later that same car pulled up into my driveway in front of the house. A woman with a New York accent and a New York license plate on her car began to gripe at me. She asked me how could I leave my dog off leash and allow him to roam. I was confused. I made this dumfounded gesture as I looked around in a 360 degree circle. "Do you see where we live?" We live on a one hundred acre ranch in the woods, why wouldn't I let him roam free? I didn't want him caged. Unfortunately he got curious and went beyond the ranch. (I am assuming.)

The lady from New York had been looking for his collar in the grass so she could identify the owner. This woman was amazing. She went to the nearest Veterinarian clinic and they refused the dog. Then she drove another twenty miles beyond that and found a Veterinarian to care for the dog. She had seen him get hit by a semi-truck. If you know anything about semis then you probably already know the dog was not going to survive. This woman was amazing! She went out of her way and not only caught the dog and picked it up, she also took the dog to a Veterinarian. She also paid the bill and she refused to let us pay her back. The Veterinarian stayed open and waited till we called. All we had to do was make the decision to put him down. There was obviously no chance for survival. We had him put down and then my husband went and picked up the dog and brought him home and buried him under a tree out back in the woods. He made sure it was deep enough so the wild hogs wouldn't dig him up. I have often wondered if he was running away from something on the ranch. He knew to stay off the highway.

We had another puppy that we rescued and he also "escaped" the ranch and ended up at the Fire Department a few miles down the road, across the highway. I often wonder if he figured out who else was living out here on the ranch and took off, running in fear of something or someone on the ranch. A neighbor claimed him and gave him to her mother in town. When we saw him in town, she was afraid we were going to take the dog back, so she claimed she bought him at a pet store. Really? There were thirteen in the litter and they all looked the same, and we had his sister Wendy. I named this dog Bo Diddley. He was so flea infested when we rescued him that he kept scratching his belly. He looked as if he was playing a guitar, hence the name Bo Diddley. Yup, that is just how I think! My husband didn't get it. He had my boys name him Lucky, since he was lucky we rescued him. I am guessing he didn't feel so lucky when he realized we had Sasquatches on the ranch. He only lasted two weeks on the ranch before he took off and found another home. I often drive by his new home just to see how he is doing. I don't get off and I don't call him. I don't want that woman to think we are trying to take him back. We were so glad he found a good home. He deserved it.

So apparently, for the first two years the animals we had were scared out of their wits of whatever was roaming around on the ranch. Remember, we were still trying to figure out what was going on and who was making all those noises and trying to scare us off the ranch. Imagine what the animals were going through? Strangely, though, the cats were not phased. They lounged around on the roof and never seemed frightened. I used to joke that Precious and her baby were living with the Sasquatches because they would disappear a week at a time. When they came back they appeared to be groomed and well fed. We couldn't imagine neighbors taking them in, they all had dogs, and they were usually viciously trained hog hunting dogs. Their dogs would have gotten to the cats and killed them before the owners did. So, they were going somewhere out there. We would see them walk out to the woods beyond the pond and lake, and when we went fishing or just walking near the pond they would show up out of nowhere. This last time that Precious showed up she was gone for four months. We assumed she had been eaten by a wild animal. Then one morning she showed up at my bedroom window, early one misty morning scratching on the glass to be let into the house. My boys screamed with excitement when they heard her. She has the most unique and delicate meow. They instinctively knew it was her. We were all happy she was home. She is a city cat, doesn't hunt, and doesn't fight. She is a very delicate house cat. That is why we named her Precious. She doesn't seem like the kind of cat that could survive in the woods. So, where does she go?

I thought this was really strange. So, I started looking up cats in ancient world mythology. In Egyptian mythology cats were worshipped and viewed as the gatekeepers to the other world, the afterlife. The first worshipped and named god in Egyptian mythology was Aker, a cat, not a domestic cat, but a large cat belonging to the feline family. At one point in ancient history killing a cat was illegal and punishable by death. I could now see why they held such positions in mythology and among the early Egyptian culture. They show little fear. Ironic how we use the term "scaredy cat". They were also worshipped and valued for their ability to take out vermin and venomous snakes. Aaaah, same reason we have so many cats on the ranch. A lot of good that does us, they spend most of their time on the roof. I also found that quite strange, since most of the unusual activity we had on the ranch, involved the roof. Hmm…, and the cats were still hanging around and didn't seemed phased by all the activity.

Wendy and Pickles, our dogs, have been with us since the first year on the ranch. They do show definite signs of stress. They used to bark all night long. Before we knew what was going on we just figured they were keeping all the wild animals away from the house. I used to laugh when ten pound Pickles, a Rat Terrier would hide in the dark corner of the garage and bark. She would bark in such a way that made her sound like a one hundred and twenty pound dog. She used the acoustics in the garage to her advantage. She sounded ferocious. Wendy is also very protective of the house and the family. She barked all the time and would go after anything that moved on the ranch. She really loves us and expresses that loyalty every day.

This year we finally realized and accepted what was going on around the ranch. Yes, it actually took us two years to get a grasp on the whole situation. (Don't judge me! I would like to see you spend a week, or one night in my shoes.) So, when we finally realized what the dogs must have been going through outside with the Sasquatches. My husband made the decision to bring the dogs inside. He purchased dog cages and set them up inside and we brought the dogs in each night. We had one dog in the dining room and one dog in the breakfast room. I also placed blankets over their cages to make them feel more secure and safer. They were so spooked by all the sounds and strange activity going on at night during the first year. We had a two car garage where they could take refuge, but that didn't seem to help. They had suffered enough. We did too. We basically didn't get any sleep for the first year and a half. This year things were going to change. We were walking into this New Third Year with our eyes wide open.

Things were finally becoming quieter on the ranch, unfortunately the dogs behaviors had not changed. They still acted as though something was outside still stalking us all the time. They reacted to every single noise. I thought that was so strange. For a while there I actually thought the Sasquatches/Bigfoots had left the ranch. We no longer had PVC pipes being thrown at the house anymore, and we no longer found turtle shells in the yard. We even went out to the bone graveyard the kids had found that first weekend on the ranch, and all the bones were gone. I haven't heard the Sasquatch/Bigfoot howls at night that we had heard during the first year, and the coyotes also stopped coming around. They used to show up at least every two weeks, and they always showed up during the full moon. Now, we heard nothing. That was until Jan the 2nd of this year. That was when I realized that the Sasquatches/Bigfoots were still here, all the time.

That was when I became keenly aware that our neighbors had not left the ranch. I am not prepared to share the whole story of the events of that night. I don't mean for this to be a tease, but seriously I think you will understand. I will share this much with you; that night they came inside the house. I was so furious, no angry, no, words cannot describe how I felt. How would you feel? My kids heard them too. This brought a whole new sense of awareness to this whole Sasquatch/Bigfoot phenomena that I was not prepared for at all. I had not heard or read anywhere in any books, blogs, or articles, of any of these creatures getting into people's houses. I had not heard or read of them coming that close to humans. Just writing this makes my heart palpitate faster and my mind starts racing and I physically feel as though I am going to burst into tears and throw up at the same time. It is an event I am not prepared to go into at this time. All I can tell you, is that they can get into the house, and that I was fit to be tied. I am a southern woman. I will defend my family with all my might. I was so mad, that I yelled at them in anger. I was physically sweating venom. I had threatened to move off the ranch and forget the whole thing. I was done with them! No more Mr. Nice Guy!! When I went to visit my mom in Dallas, my brother gave me a shot gun and a box of shells. When I got home I enrolled in a gun class for women. That is how scared I was. I was prepared to move and I was prepared to defend my family if I was put in that position.

This is where the new puppy comes into the story. They knew I was mad. They knew I was serious. I honestly think the new puppy was a gift. Those of you who are Bigfoot savvy know exactly what I am talking about. Right? This was their way of smoothing things over with me. And it worked. I accepted our new reality and I accepted the new gift. I had to accept the fact that they have the ability to get into the house and I had to get over it. I had to also realize that despite the new eerily quiet atmosphere on the ranch, they were definitely still here. They hadn't gone anywhere.

Why do I call Sparky the Sasquatch's puppy? Well, remember how scared all the other dogs were? Well, by this time we were bringing Wendy and Pickles inside every night to sleep in blanket covered cages. Sparky/Spartacus on the other hand, wanted to sleep outside. This seemed very odd. He actually wanted to sleep outside. And guess what? He never barked at night. He was never scared. Then the balls started showing up again, tennis balls and baseballs. Just today I was coaching my sons at the local high school tennis courts, and I was shocked by how full the ball hopper was. I had a hard time closing it. That means we have extra balls in the ball hopper that are not mine. Guess what else? He can fetch!! He absolutely loves it here on the ranch!! The second we let him out in the morning he heads out to the pond for his morning swim. Sparky is having a very different experience here on the ranch than all the other dogs have had. It all makes sense. The Sasquatches/Bigfoots are not trying to scare us or the animals off the ranch anymore. Lucky Sparky is having a very positive experience on the ranch, which makes me wonder if he is aware of the other creatures. I have noticed him staring up into the trees and into the woods. He plays and chases things all the time. He is having the time of his life. Very different from before. One night when I was brave enough to sit out on the patio, I noticed him looking up in the trees at something. What he sees, I can only guess. Considering his confidence and lack of fear, I believe he has a much different relationship with the Sasquatches.

Chapter Three
DAWN Goes Missing

I think someone was playing with Sparky. I
think he saw and heard someone in the trees. I
wouldn't even doubt it if they were calling his
name as they like to call my boys by their names.
Then one day I noticed that a brand new two
pound pack of ham was missing from the
refrigerator. I was so upset. I had just bought it
the day before. I had planned to divide the pack
and store the individual packs in the freezer. At
first I was angry with the boys. I couldn't
understand how they could eat a two pound pack

of ham in one day. I mean, after all we have to watch our nickels and dimes too. I had just made the decision to stay home this next year so I could write full time and be here for the boys. I also wanted to have more time to explore, investigate, research and figure out what was happening on the ranch. All of this meant we were going to be taking a financial hit. My income would drastically decrease by more than 85%.

Yes. Don't be fooled. This is not some huge money making venture for me or any other Habituators out there. We are personally spending more money on repairs. Just this week we had to call the property manager out, and she called the plumber. We had another pipe break outside. That means gallons and gallons of water were flooding the pasture making a river into the woods. This time the property manager had the plumber incase the main faucet in cement and then she decided to have all the other faucets replaced and secured above ground by incasing them in cement as well. The plumber also found a shut off valve closer to the house and placed a covering on it for easier access. No more driving down the road in the middle of the night looking in the dense woods under the huge oak tree, for the main shut off valve. This one was right next to the house and under a light. We have three other doors to replace as well. The dogs have destroyed the door in the garage that leads to the laundry room. They were so frightened by something outside that they shredded the exterior side of that door. They have also destroyed the patio screen door. They ran right through that door running for their lives as if they were being chased. I also plan to purchase iron screen mesh doors to protect the new doors. Remember in the Memories book, the front Oak door still has cracks in it from something huge throwing itself up against that door on New Year's Eve. While I was walking around the house assessing all the damage, I realized the front door at one time had an exterior storm door or glass door, and that is gone. So could it be that others before us have had the same issue with animals tearing through doors? So, things are tight, we can't afford to make all of these repairs and also have food disappear and walk out the door. I bet you thought I was crazy when I told you my dishes were missing in the last book. Well, now we all know how they were getting my dishes.

By the way, I did finally tell the property manager about all the activity around the house. I had a book signing and I was prepared in case she showed up. I began to read the chapter where I am describing her. She leaned in and asked, "Is that why everybody left?" I was stunned! Yup! Then she mentioned that the new renter down the road on the other side of the ranch was having strange activity also. That renter had just decided that her house was haunted. My property manager is so classy. She wanted me to clear something up.

Even though the other renters left in a hurry and with no notice, she did manage to give them their deposit back even though they had left the ranch and broken the lease. Such class! So, with this new knowledge, that is why she decided to secure all the water faucets outside.

So, back to the ham. No, I know that this seems so insignificant. I finally decided that the Baby Sasquatches were coming in and helping themselves to the ham. The bread started going missing as well. Then I came to the conclusion that there was another reason Sparky liked being outside so much. I think they were feeding him ham at night. Then a few weeks later the alarm on the upright freezer was set off. We would wake up in the morning and the alarm would be going off. We couldn't hear it at night since all the rooms are so far from the laundry room. The freezer is also right next to the door that leads to the garage. It is also one of the doors that needs to be replaced and is torn to shreds from the outside. The inside of the door is still intact. This freezer is kind of fancy. It has a computer on the door. It monitors the temperature, moisture and other stuff. It also beeps if the door is ajar. The alarm was claiming the door was ajar every morning we woke up, for a whole week. We kept moving things around trying to figure out what was blocking the door and setting off the sensor. Nothing was blocking the door. Yet, the sensor kept going off. This happened the exact same time the food started going missing. I have noticed frozen vegetables and loaves of frozen bread missing from the freezer. I am not accusing anyone of anything, I am just reporting the facts.

Here is a picture of the laundry room/garage entrance.

Figure 1 Exterior Garage Door in shreds.

[I am using this picture to give you an idea of the destruction. The animals clawed three layer off this door. This is the door I am replacing.]

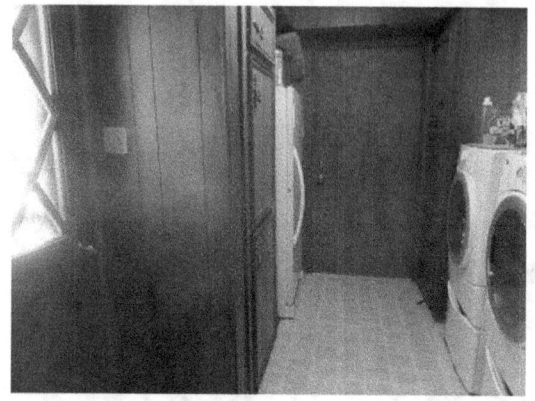

Figure 2 Garage Interior Door to Laundry Room

[This picture shows you the laundry room/pantry. Notice the deep freezer on the left. It is right next to the garage entrance. The other door on the left with windows is the back door that leads to the driveway. There are two entrances to this room. Easily accessible and right next to the food. Easy in, easy out.]

A few weeks after the ham incident, I was looking for DAWN dish soap. I had just purchased several bottles. Knowing that I would soon be out of work and staying home, I consciously began to stock up on food and necessities. Therefore, I was also stocking up on dish soap. So, I had just bought three bottles of DAWN. I loved the new scents. There was a tropical pink soap, a lavender purple, and a yellow pineapple. This week for example, I bought another bottle of green soap that smelled like cantaloupe and cucumber. Yes, I am crazy about the new scents. I used to have a business making homemade soaps. I still have over two hundred fragrances, and I still make soaps for special occasions and special people. I made chocolate dipped strawberry hearts for my sons' teachers for Valentines. Then I made soaps for Mother's Day for a Women's Bible Study Group. I mostly make them as gifts. I don't think people really want to pay $8.00 for a bar of soap anymore. So, call me crazy, this is my one vice. I love the different scents that DAWN is now putting on the market. This is why I knew the bottles were missing, and I knew which ones and what scents they were. I was baffled. I stood there in complete shock, going over the entire scenario in my head. I was trying to figure out who took my new bottles of soap and why. The other reason I use DAWN dish soap is that I use it on the cats. It is safe to use on animals and it kills fleas on contact. DAWN dish soap is used to safely wash off the animals that survived the oil spills. So, if it is safe enough for them, it should be safe enough for my cats and dogs. Right?

These are the moments that make you question your sanity. However, it is obvious that I am aware of every little detail, so they can't put one past me. I knew my dish soap was missing and I knew someone had taken it, or "borrowed" it. (My sons wanted me to use the word borrowed!)

It was another one of those defining moments, just like the first night we heard the one thousand pound creature on the roof. We just stood there in shock, looking at each other. Self-evaluating, assessing all the information, going over details in my head, and realizing other things are missing as well. Then eventually we go about our business and just accept what we have absolutely no control over. I was literally throwing my hands up in the air. I was helpless. What could I do? Yes, call the police and report missing ham, bread, and dish soap? I could give them my drawing of the suspect and explain my theories as to how I believed a Sasquatch was coming into my house and taking things from the refrigerator, freezer and cabinet under the sink. Do you understand? That is why I tell people that 99% of eyewitnesses do not report Bigfoot sightings or activity. There is absolutely nothing you can do! Who would believe such a thing? Well believe it! It happened, and it ain't over!

Susan Sullivan

Chapter Four
Why Do They Need
My DAWN?

Okay, I can't help but insert my humor. By now you have discovered that I do have a healthy sense of humor when it comes to the Sasquatches. Well, I have a sense of humor concerning everything. I can't take life seriously anymore. This, least of all. So, my first response to the situation was obvious. Remember, they had already "borrowed" my dishes. So, I have to admit for a minute there I thought, do they need dish soap to wash their new dishes? Hey, it could happen. After all they are observing us all the time. I have two kitchen windows above the sink. I am sure they see me all the time through the window doing what I am doing all the time, washing dishes. It makes perfect sense, and I am all about making sense of all of this. Nothing mystical or magical going on here. They have taken my dishes, now they are taking my dish soap. I jokingly commented to my husband, to keep an eye on the pond for telltale signs of suds.

What was so frustrating about all of this is that I was in the middle of doing dishes. I also had a new barbeque grill and I was needing to clean a dirty crusty grill before barbecuing again. Dawn is perfect for this job, it cuts the grease and cleans the grills perfectly. I wanted to smoke a brisket that very day, and I was needing to prepare the grill. I was angry and frustrated because I go to great lengths to plan things out. I also like to stock up on items. Remember, we live twenty five miles from the nearest major grocery store. We just don't drop everything and get in the car and run to the store to get another bottle of dish soap. Doesn't happen here. So, you can imagine my frustration when I realized that not just one bottle of dish soap was missing, but three bottles! Why?

After searching the kitchen the pantry and laundry room, we then turned to the guest bathroom, and found nothing. I then remembered to look under my bathroom sink and I found one loan bottle. This bottle was different though. It was not a typical bottle of dish soap. It was dish soap, but in a fancy square bottle with a pump. It wasn't labeled with the words "DAWN" like the other bottles. So, why did they leave this bottle of dish soap? Could it be that the different bottle, somehow threw them off? Were they specifically looking for this specific brand? Are they really that smart and discerning? See, I am always thinking, always trying to solve this mystery. I think, then rethink and go over it again. I am like a detective. I plan to figure this out, the who, they why, they when, and the where of it all.

Chapter Five
Putting Two And Two Together

Putting this all together. First of all let me explain why I have a bottle of DAWN dish soap under my bathroom sink and why I placed it in a square bottle. I use DAWN dish soap to bathe the cats. I don't like the over the counter flea shampoos. I have had two puppies die in years past after bathing them with a flea shampoo. The cats roam the ranch and are picking up all sorts of fleas and ticks. I want to bathe them with something that is safe. I believe DAWN is safe to use, since as I mentioned before, it appears to be safe enough to treat sea animals and birds drenched in oil by oil spills.

The reason I used the square bottle with a pump is easy to explain. Have you ever bathed a cat? All claws are out. You have to have both hands ready and available. One hand is holding all four paws while the free hand is pumping the soap out of the square bottle and lathering the cat up. The square bottle is harder to topple over while struggling with a screaming, clawing, soaking wet cat. Cats don't like water, they don't like soap, and they don't like to be held down. So, bathing a cat is a battle. Now try bathing ten cats, five of them kittens. Aah I see the light coming on. It does make sense.

Now, why would the Sasquatches need my DAWN soap? Well, I still wasn't sure. After all, I don't bathe the cats outside. I bathe them in my bathtub. They have never seen me bathe the cats. If they had, they would know what I was using the dish soap for and for what purpose. I would totally understand that. But, that didn't happen.

So, two weeks went by and I had bought more dish soap. Another bottle went missing. Then I turned to my husband while I was standing at the kitchen sink, recounting all the events, the missing food and another bottle missing. With a huge audible sigh, I realized we now have to accept that they can get into the house. All though the thought of them using my dish soap on their "new" dishes was funny and was plausible, it just didn't make sense to me. And why four bottles now? They didn't have that many dishes. There must be another reason. What is so special and so important that they must come into my house at night and steal my dish soap? It was at this very moment I realized why the other renters before us had all fled with such fear and in such a hurry. This is why they thought the house was haunted. Someone was getting into the house.

Still standing at the kitchen sink and
realizing another bottle was missing, I went over
the events with my husband, explaining the one
bottle that was left behind in the bathroom, and
how I used that specific bottle on the cats to rid
them of fleas. I explained why I specifically used
this brand of soap. Then I could see it right before
my eyes. The light went on and somebody was
home. I saw the look of realization and total
awareness in my husband's eyes and the look and
expression was priceless. He then bolted out of the
kitchen and briskly walked to the garage. He
brought in an old grass and mud covered empty
soap bottle and placed it on the kitchen counter. I
could see he had put it all together. It was the
most amazing moment. The skeptic was finally
putting two and two together. I asked him where
he had found the empty bottle. He said, "The
garage." Then, as if I was the lead investigator on
an episode CSI Miami, I continued to question, no
more like interrogate my husband. I then asked,

"When was the last time you used the dish soap, and where?" He slowly and clearly described the scene as if he was on trial for his life. (Not really, I am just using my creative license here! See, I can't take anything seriously!) He continued by explaining the last time he had used the dish soap. It had been two weeks since he had used the last bottle of dish soap. Sparky, the new puppy, who was now a growing vivacious trouble making three and half month old black lab(thank God he didn't turn out to be a Pit Bull) had been sprayed by a skunk. Instead of taking him to my bathroom and bathing him in my bathtub, my husband decided to get a metal tub and bathe the dog outside in the yard with DAWN dish soap.

He said the smell was so bad, he didn't dare attempt to bathe Sparky inside, or even bring the dog inside. In my opinion, someone else outside, on the ranch was watching all of these events transpire. My husband went ahead and bathed the other two dogs, since all the necessary supplies and equipment were available. He usually bathes the dogs inside in my bathtub, in my bathroom. It is easier to confine them to the bathroom while they dry off.

Are you with me? Whoever is out there observing everything we do, was also observing my husband bathing the dogs. I bet they also witnessed Sparky's encounter with the skunk. I also have to wonder how many times they have encountered these same smelly creatures and how many times they have been sprayed. I have to wonder if it was the momma Squatch who stood out there in the trees as my husband so carefully bathed the dogs. I can only imagine she was taking it all in, and learning. She was also putting two and two together, and figured out what we us to rid the dogs of the horrible awful skunk smell and the fleas and the ticks. Can you imagine? How do they clean that dark heavy long hairy coat? How do they keep from getting fleas and ticks?

In my opinion, I believe she did what any good mother would do. She ordered the little ones to wait till the dead of night when we were fast asleep, to go inside and steal every bottle of DAWN we had. Now that makes perfect sense! I also understand why they needed so many bottles. It wasn't for the dishes, it was for them. Oh I bet they smell pretty now. So, if you are walking in the woods and you get a waft of lavender, pomegranate, cucumber melon, or Hawaiian pineapple, you can thank me for introducing the lovely scents to the Bigfoot people. Could that be why we haven't smelled the pungent odor of the Big Daddy recently? I wonder if she ordered him to take a bath. Hmm…Cucumber Melon maybe?

Chapter Six
My Response

So, I bet you are wondering, what my response was after realizing these creatures had the ability to get inside the house and take whatever they wanted? Well, I went right to the grocery store and bought the biggest bottle of dish soap. Unfortunately, I did not buy DAWN dish soap. Remember, we are counting our nickels and dimes like everyone else. I bought the cheaper generic brand. Guess what? It is still there under the sink. It doesn't say DAWN on it. Picky, Picky, Picky. So I bought smaller bottles of DAWN that are in a blue basket under the sink, while I continue to use the generic brand. My, what I will do for our Sasquatches.

I purchased a new door for the laundry room to replace the one that was torn to shreds. I am also ordering the steel mesh doors for the other entrances. I am looking for fruit trees that we can plant around the ranch so the Sasquatches can enjoy fruit long after we are gone. And we just continue to go about our normal everyday lives and accept the creatures that live just beyond the backyard, beyond the trees and beyond the ranch somewhere out there.

Author's Notes

I hope you enjoyed this short story. It is based solely on actual events. I know it is hard to believe. That is exactly why I feel the need to share my experiences. I wouldn't believe it either, but I have to since it is actually happening to me. I am constantly amazed by the new things we are experiencing and discovering about these creatures. If you enjoyed this short story, you will be happy to know there are more to come.

www.ingramcontent.com/pod-product-compliance
Lightning Source LLC
Chambersburg PA
CBHW070624290526
45790CB00002B/981